The Genuine And Apocryphal Gospels Compared

Samuel Butler

The Genuine and Apocryphal Gospels compared.

A

CHARGE,

DELIVERED TO THE

CLERGY OF THE ARCHDEACONRY OF DERBY,

AT THE

Visitations at Derby and Chesterfield,

JUNE 6 & 7, 1822,

AND PUBLISHED AT THEIR REQUEST.

BY SAMUEL BUTLER, D.D. F.R.S. & S.A. &c.

ARCHDEACON OF DERBY,

AND HEAD MASTER OF SHREWSBURY SCHOOL.

SHREWSBURY:

PRINTED BY WILLIAM EDDOWES, SALOPIAN JOURNAL OFFICE;

AND SOLD BY LONGMAN, HURST, REES, ORME, AND BROWN, LONDON;
AND H. MOZLEY, DERBY.

1822.

IN the following pages there are two arguments which bear a close affinity to those adduced by Mr. Rennell in his " Proofs of Inspiration." One of them relates to the manner in which the books of the New Testament were collected; the other to the inferences drawn from a comparison between the genuine and apocryphal Gospels.

The Author of this Charge feels it right to state, that it was written long before Mr. Rennell's book was published, and that he never saw that work till he was on the very point of proceeding to hold his Visitation. He was, however, much gratified in finding his own views of the subject confirmed, by so striking and wholly accidental a coincidence with those of the acute and able Christian Advocate.

Should any apology be necessary for the delay between the delivery of this Charge and its publication, the Author begs leave to say, that he has been absent from England from the time of his Visitation to the beginning of the present month.

In deference to the opinion of the Clergy of the Archdeaconry, who conceived that a cheap edition of this Charge would be useful, the Author has caused it to be printed also in the octavo form for general circulation.

Shrewsbury, August 7, 1822.

A

CHARGE,

&c.

My Reverend Brethren,

On my introduction to you last year, it seemed expedient that I should enter into those matters which are immediately connected with the office I have to discharge among you; that I should explain to you my views and expectations on that subject, and express those wishes, which I most deeply feel, to promote on all occasions the interests of religion and the Established Church, and your own personal comforts and convenience as far as they are any way connected with my jurisdiction.

I said, on that occasion, all that appeared to me so connected as to be inseparable from the topic I had chosen. Something remained, relative to the *internal*, if I may be allowed to refer what I then said to the *external* concerns of the church; which I had intended to reserve for our present assembling; but circumstances have occurred which induce me to defer this discussion to some future period (as it may be taken up with propriety at any time), and at present lead me to call your attention to a different subject.

Before I enter upon this, however, I cannot but notice the heavy loss which this Deanery, and in particular the place where we are now assembled, has sustained since our last meeting. In one case, a venerable member of our society, full of years and good deeds, whose beneficence was as unbounded as his means were extensive, and whose charities were as much beyond the measure of ordinary bounty, as his years were beyond the ordinary period of human existence, has been gathered, at an almost patriarchal age, like a ripe shock of corn, to the harvest of the blessed. In the other, one of the most useful and most exemplary of our brethren, whose loss will be long, and deeply, and generally deplored, and the remembrance of whose zeal and virtues will be, piously and affectionately cherished in this extensive parish, of which he was forty years the diligent and faithful pastor, has been called to his great reward. Let our regret for the loss of these good men be mitigated, by our reliance on the promises made to such faithful servants by our Saviour in his Gospel: *We sorrow not as men without hope, for those that go hence in the Lord.* We rest our own eternal hopes, on living as they have lived, on departing hence as they have departed. Let us be consoled in our christian pilgrimage by this faith, and animated by these examples.*

None of you can be ignorant of the attempts which from time to time have been made, and are still making, to propagate infidel doctrines. Religion itself, its ordinances and its ministers, have been attacked with a degree of active hostility, which has seldom been equalled, never surpassed, and which, while it shews the earnestness of our antagonists, betrays also their consciousness of our strength and importance as teachers and guardians of our flocks. But besides the direct and open warfare thus carried on against religion, a more secret and insidious mode of attack has been resorted to by some of its adversaries, who endeavour to sap the very foundations of our faith; and to lessen the confidence and veneration of mankind for the Holy Scripiures, by variously directed attempts to weaken their authority ; it being evident to these men, that if they can undermine the very foundation of our faith, the superstructure that is built on it must inevitably fall.

Among the most insidious of these attacks is a publication entitled " The Apocryphal New Testament," which appeared

* This part of the Charge, which was delivered at Chesterfield only, alludes to the death of those excellent men, the Rev. Francis Gisborne, the munificent Rector of Staveley, aged upwards of ninety, and the Rev. George Bossley, so beloved in the extensive parish of Chesterfield, of which he was forty years the faithful minister, that his parishioners, with a feeling truly honourable to him and to themselves, went into general mourning on his decease.

in the course of last year, the obvious intention of which is, to throw a degree of doubt and uncertainty on those books of the New Testament, which we receive as genuine and canonical.

Now though I feel a perfect assurance that every one of you, my Reverend Brethren, is impressed with a conviction of the truth and authenticity of those sacred records, which you have solemnly declared that you believe, and on which you rest the very grounds of your faith; though I have also no doubt that you feel it your duty, and in conformity with that duty ARE *ready at all times, to give an answer to every man that asketh you a reason of the hope that is in you;* still the subject to which I have alluded is so important, the poison intended to be disseminated is contained in so small and tangible a compass, and the antidotes to that poison in so wide a range, and, generally speaking, so much out of the way of a parochial clergyman's library, that I trust I shall not be doing an unacceptable service, if I make these Apocryphal gospels the subject of my present observations.

In order to do this with effect, I must just glance at the grounds which we have for the authenticity of those books of the New Testament which we actually receive. Our enquiry need not go farther, because the books of the Old Testament are not impugned by the publication in question, and are acknowledged as genuine by the greatest adversaries of Christianity, in whose keeping they have been.

The evidence, then, for the canonical books of the New Testament may be considered either as external or internal.

The external evidence may be divided into direct, traditional, and inferential.

By the direct evidence, I mean that immediate and historical proof which we receive from those authors whose writings have come down to us; these are principally the Fathers of the church, in whose writings the books of the New Testament are incessantly quoted, so that even the whole text of Scripture might be recovered, from them, were all the copies of the New Testament destroyed.

By the traditional, I mean that of authors who have not come down to us, but whose testimony has been quoted by those who have—such are frequently mentioned in the writings of the Fathers.

By the inferential, I mean that of heretics who admitted some portions of scripture and rejected others, as the Ebionites, or who altered the sacred text in some parts and retained it in others, as the Marcionites, because they at least bear testimony to the *existence* of those parts of scripture which they reject or alter; besides these there are certain opponents of Christianity, such as Porphyry and Celsus, who on the same ground, as far as we have any fragments of them, become valuable and important witnesses to the *existence* of the sacred text; to these we must add the various early versions of the New Testament, which, being of themselves of most remote antiquity, and capable of being traced up to the beginning of the second, and perhaps even to the first century after Christ, are yet confessedly less antient than the writings of which they profess to be translations. There are also various other critical and historical testimonies which fall under this division.

By the internal evidence, I mean such as may be derived from the Scriptures themselves relative to their authenticity, which is resolvable either into matters of doctrine, or matters of opinion, or matters of fact.

It is quite impossible, within the limits of an address like the present, to enter into the details of this evidence, and indeed it is also quite unnecessary. The defences of the authenticity of the sacred books are so numerous and so excellent, and I may add so familiar, not only to the clergy but to the great portion of the laity who are capable of understanding them, that it is quite superfluous to undertake a new one. It may be sufficient to have reminded you of the principal heads of this evidence, because they are most convincing and satisfactory when applied to the genuine scriptures, and are perfectly inapplicable to the spurious ones. The direct evidence for these spurious gospels is exceedingly scanty and feeble, the traditional far more so, and the inferential decisively contra-dictory to their authenticity. As to the internal evidence for the truth of these writings, they are in themselves so childish and absurd, so contradictory to all our ideas of the divine attributes, so derogatory to the Majesty of the Deity, so totally unedifying for any purposes of religious, or moral, or social life, so undoctrinal and unconsolatory, that they carry their own confutation within them, and can never gain credit with any person of sober sense and judgment. The evil which they can produce, considered in themselves, is trifling, for they give no grounds for action, present no articles of faith, lay down no rule of life and manners. The great danger is from *the mode of their publication*, the intention of which, under the specious appearance of candour and learning, is evidently of the most mischievous and malevolent kind. It is to the prefaces and arrangement of these apocryphal gospels, and to the form and language of the translation, that I shall principally direct your attention, because in these the essence of the poison is contained.

I need not remind you that these writings were collected and published in their original languages by the very learned John Albert Fabricius, in the year 1719, under the Title of Codex Apocryphus Novi Testamenti, as a supplement to the Codex Pseudepigraphus Veteris Testamenti, first published by the same scholar in 1713.

That learned and excellent editor, when collecting these writings from various quarters, had certainly no intention of impugning the sacred volume, which contains the genuine word of God. He conceived, and justly, that in thus bringing together these scattered remnants of idleness, ignorance or heresy, illustrating and refuting them by the criticisms of professedly the greatest scholars, and confining the whole to the use of the learned by leaving them in their original tongues, he was doing no disservice to the cause of Christianity, but an acceptable work to those whose own faith is too well founded to be shaken, and who know how to extract healing ‘medicines from the rankest weeds, and to confirm the faith of others, by turning the weapons of their enemies upon themselves.

How far the English editor appears to have had the same intention will be submitted to your judgment in the sequel. That *ostensible* editor is a man whose name is but too well known to the ranks of disaffection and infidelity; who appears to possess talents above the ordinary class, and effrontery much above those talents. . Still, with shrewdness which leads him easily to catch the suggestions of subtler spirits than his own, and with steadiness of purpose which induces him to persevere in the course he has adopted, the book under our consideration undoubtedly is not, and in fact does not assume to be, his own production. I grieve to say that the *real* editor is a man of talents and attainments which qualify him for undertaking better things, and is therefore entitled to no quarter for wilful and deliberate perversion of the truth.

I shall now proceed to an investigation of the prefaces, and touch upon such other parts of the work as appear to require more particular notice. I must however premise, that the thought of thus undermining Christianity by placing before the common people spurious Gospels, as like in form and phraseology as they can be made, to the originals, is an English improvement upon a French invention.' I have in my possession a French translation of these very writings, but not in Scriptural phraseology, published, evidently with the same insidious intention, professedly at London, but in fact at Paris 1769; the work I believe is not common.

The English translation now under our consideration has seen two editions in the space of a short time. The preface to the first edition begins with the following question, and remark.

' " After the writings contained in the New Testament were selected from the numerous Gospels and Epistles then in existence, what became of the books that were rejected by the compilers ?"' " This question naturally occurs on every investigation as to the period when, and the persons by whom, the New Testament was formed. It has been supposed by many, that the volume was compiled by the first council of Nice, which was held early in the fourth century."

Now this question, and the remark on it, natural and simple as they appear, contain several insidious positions.

First, it is taken for granted, that the writings of the New Testament *were compiled or selected*, by a certain set of persons, from numerous gospels and epistles in existence at the time this *compilation* or *selection* was made.

c

Secondly, it is insinuated that they were compiled by the first council of Nice, that is to say, not till between three and four hundred years after the birth of Christ, which council is in the subsequent paragraphs held up to the most marked derision and contempt.

Now with regard to the first position, it may be observed, that there is no sort of proof that the writings of the New Testament WERE *selected* from the numerous Gospels and Epistles then in existence. It is one thing to COL*lect* and another to SE*lect*, and it seems highly probable that the writings of the New Testament were COL*lected*, not SE*lected*.

It is consonant to reason, that as fast as the genuine epistles and gospels were written by those whose names they bear, they would be added to the code of Scripture which already existed in those churches to which they were addressed, and that they would be communicated by the Bishops and elders of those churches, to the neighbouring Christian churches, and by those again to others, and thus authentic copies would be dispersed through the Christian world; and a COL*lection* of the sacred books would thus be made by degrees in every Christian Church, as fast as the genuine and properly authenticated scriptures were communicated to it. Such *collection* therefore, would be made by progressive additions of genuine and authorised books, not by SE*lections* of what appeared to be best, from a number which were acknowledged to be bad. And as this is, á priori, consonant to reason, so also do we find it confirmed by enquiry into fact. It is quite clear, from the command of St. Paul, that the authentic scriptures actually were thus circulated in the churches.

"*And when this Epistle is read among you,* says he to the Colossians iv. 16, *cause that it be read also in the church of the Laodiceans, and that ye likewise read the epistle from Laodicea,* meaning most probably the Epistle to the Ephesians, a copy of which, sent to Laodicea, was to be forwarded to Colossæ.

Again we find St. Peter ii. III. 16, and St. James plainly, though not in express words, almost through the whole of his second chapter, referring to the Epistles of St. Paul. Now as these Epistles of St. James and St. Peter are not addressed to any particular churches, but are what are called *catholic* or *general* Epistles, it is fairly to be inferred, that in the days of these Apostles, they knew that their own Epistles would be sent from church to church till they became *generally received,* and knew also that the Epistles of St. Paul were *generally received* in like manner.

In this way we may conceive the whole of the sacred books to have been originally *collected;* gospel after gospel and epistle after epistle being added, as fast as they were received, either from the original writers or from the heads of the respective churches to which they were originally addressed; and thus a *collection* will have been made, in a manner worthy the dignity

and importance of the subject; not a *selection* from a number
of promiscuous and unauthenticated writings, in which, according
to the common acceptation of the term (and, I have no doubt,
according to its *intended* signification in this instance) the choice
may have been influenced by caprice, directed by fraud, or
misled by error.

It should be here observed, that the above remarks apply to the
original mode in which the New Testament was collected. I am
well aware of the controversies which subsequently originated
with the heretics in the third and fourth centuries, and which led
some of the Fathers of the Church to adopt a looser mode of
expression when speaking of these books, and to divide them
into ὁμολογύμινα, or books acknowledged by all, which contain all
the Gospels, the Acts, and St. Paul's Epistles, 1st Peter, and 1st
John; ἀϑιλιγόμινα, γνωριμὰ δὲ ὅμως τοῖς πολλοῖς, that is, books controverted
by some, but generally acknowledged as genuine, comprising the
other five Catholic Epistles and Apocalypse; arid νόθα or spurious,
such as the Epistle of Barnabas, the Revelation of Peter, &c.
But in fact, when the controversy had first been started by the
heretics, it was almost impossible for the defenders of the New
Testament to avoid using such terms. Indeed the argument,
instead of making against the prior establishment of the present code
of scripture, is strongly in its favour. For, first, it necessarily
presupposes all the present canonical books to be more antient
than the controversy respecting their genuineness. Secondly, it
admits that the generality of Christians received the canonical
books as we receive them; thirdly, that the genuineness of only

a very small part of the present code of Scripture was ever questioned; and fourthly, that the code of Scripture was not larger in the early ages than it is at present, but that the books we still consider as spurious (and possibly several more) were then also looked upon in the same light.

The editor of the Apocryphal New Testament insinuates, that the present *Selection*, as he calls it, was made at the first council of Nice, which was held in the fourth century, about A.D. 325. He afterwards, however, in conformity with what I have just alleged, with an appearance of candour, observes, "Although it is uncertain whether the books of the New Testament were declared canonical by the Nicene council, or by some other, or when or by whom they were collected into a volume, it is certain that they were considered genuine and authentic, with a few variations of opinion as to some of them, by the most early Christian writers, and that they were *selected* from various other gospels and epistles, the titles of which are mentioned in the works of the Fathers and early historians of the church." He then proceeds thus—" The books that exist, of those not included in the canon, are carefully brought together into the present volume. They naturally assume the title of the Apocryphal New Testament, *and he who possesses this* AND *the New Testament has,* IN THE TWO VOLUMES, *a collection of all the historical records relative to Christ and his Apostles now in existence, and considered sacred* BY CHRISTIANS *during the first four centuries after Christ.*"* In a note on this passage the writer adds, "Of

* There is no difference of type in the preface from which I have made this quotation.

course the Ebionites and various other sects, denominated heretics
by the Fathers and Councils, are included in the denomination
of *Christians*."

I have already shewn that the New Testament was probably
a *collection*, not a *selection*, and our adversary admits that " the
books it contains were considered as genuine and authentic, with
a few variations of opinion as to some of them, by the most
early Christian writers ;" but he evidently wishes to insinuate
that they were not *selected* till the Council of Nice in A. D. 325.

Now it is clearly demonstrated by Mosheim, p. 48, and
Michaelis, vol. 1, p. 32, &c.* (two of the highest authorities we
can have) that before the first half of the second century had

---

* See also Mill. Prolegom. p. 23, § 196, who thinks the Collection originated
with the Church at Rome, and shews that it *must* have existed before A. D. 127,
and probably was made about A. D. 110, or earlier, the *gospels* having been
collected about A. D. 99, and a collection of Apostolic Epistles having been made
before A. D. 94. Lardner observes (Hist. of the Apostles, &c. vol. 1, p. 49) that
" before the end of the first century, yea not very long after the middle of it, it is
likely there were Collections made of the four Gospels and most of the other books
of the New Testament, which were in the hands of a good number of churches
and persons." He adds, p. 50, that " this canon was not determined by the
authority of Councils. But the books of which it consists are known to be the
genuine writings of the Apostles and Evangelists in the same way and manner
that we know the works of Cæsar, Cicero, Virgil, Horace, Tacitus, to be theirs.
And the canon has been formed upon the ground of an unanimous or generally
concurring testimony and tradition." I hope no one will imagine that, having
mentioned Mill and Lardner in this note for the sake of quotation, I consider
them as inferior to Mosheim and Michaelis whom I have referred to in the text.

elapsed, that is to say, near two hundred years before the first general Council of Nice, the code of the New Testament, as we now have it, with the exception perhaps in some churches of the ἀντιλεγόμενα above-mentioned, that is to say, five Catholic Epistles and the Revelations, was received in all churches through the whole Christian world. It is therefore certain that the Sacred Volume either wholly, or at least in all its essential parts, was *collected* before any part of this Apocryphal New Testament, except *possibly** the first Epistle of Clement to the Corinthians, was in existence. And this is a fact of great importance, inasmuch as it proves that the *selection*, as the editor calls it, of the genuine scriptures, if made at all, must have been made from very different documents from those now brought forward. But though it is certain that at a very early period there were various false documents in existence, and that many of the early heretics altered the real text of the New Testament to suit their own particular views and opinions, I have already given my reasons for believing that the sacred volume was never *selected* at all, and that the *collection* having been made in the way I have explained, the orthodox churches rejected these spurious writings without putting them in competition with the standard books. For instance, they did not select the four received Gospels from the Protevangelion, the Gospels of Infancy, and the Gospel of Nicodemus, declaring the one set genuine and the other spurious; but having already the four received Gospels, they of course rejected all the others as spurious and unauthenticated.

---

* I say *possibly* to obviate all cavil, but have no doubt myself on the subject.

We must not pass over another expression in the same para-graph, that " he who possesses the genuine and Apocryphal New Testaments, *has in the two volumes a collection of all the historical* RECORDS relative to Christ and his Apostles now in existence, and considered sacred *by Christians*, during the first ages of Christi-anity." This is evidently an attempt to place the historical authority of the genuine and Apocryphal New Testaments on equal terms, by insinuating that both are *equally historical records*. Now a record is *an* AUTHENTIC *memorial*. A *forged* decree or treaty, therefore, cannot be justly called an *historical record*. No historian of sense or honesty will knowingly appeal to it, and the very use of such a phrase is a contradiction in terms. But the intention in using it is obvious, as is also that of the other insidious expression, " considered as sacred *by Christians*," to explain which we are told in a note that " of course the Ebionites and various other sects denominated heretics by the fathers and councils, are included in the denomination of *Christians*."* That is to say, the great body of sober and pious believers in the Christian church, who received the canonical scriptures as we have from them received them, have no juster claim to the title of Christians, than every class of heretics, however wild and impious their tenets, however avowed and acknowledged their corruptions of the sacred text. If good faith had been intended by the editor, it is so obvious that he should at least have written ' considered as sacred by any sect of Christ-ians,' that it is impossible to read the passage and have any doubt as to his design.

---

* The word *Christians* is printed in Italics in the Note.

I pass over the remainder of the prefaces, which are written with an affectation of candour and moderation to which every man of common discernment will know what credit he should attribute. I pass over also the hackneyed cant of declamation against " the bloodshed and cruelties perpetrated in the name of Christianity ;" against " mystifying Fathers and Councils ;" " Soldier kings ;" " primitive simplicity ;" and " the happy " time" " when every man will be a priest unto himself." I pass over the equally hackneyed scorn and defiance of bigots, shrinemakers, malignants, and persecutors ; these are phrases of course, which make up the stock in trade of all such enlighteners of mankind, and I come to the tables and prefaces to the several books, which require some observations.

Immediately before the books of the Apocryphal New Testament is a table, containing the order of them, and made to resemble, as closely as possible, the table of the books of canonical scripture. Thus, " Mary hath Chapters 8," meaning that the Gospel of the Birth of Mary hath eight Chapters. " Protevangelion hath Chapters 26 ;" and so of the rest. The object here is precisely the same as that of the translation, to bring these spurious books to as close an exterior conformity as possible to the received books of the New Testament, for the purpose of elevating the one and depreciating the other. A third column follows, citing the authorities. It is impossible to go through them all within the limits of an address like the present ; an examination of the two first may suffice.

D

It is said in this table that the Gospel of Mary is preserved in the works of St. Jerome. *Preserved in the works of St. Jerome!* The editor of these spurious writings is too well read in their history not to know, that by the unanimous consent of all scholars and competent judges, the insertion of this Gospel among the works of St. Jerome /has been admitted to be an infamous forgery. Erasmus observes that the style is so unlike Jerome's, that the most unlettered might detect it. Casaubon gives us the name of the forger of these books, one Seleucus, sometimes called Leucius, a noted heretic among the Manicheans. Petavius calls him (in coarse words, it must be owned) an impudent liar. Vossius has the same remark; and our own very learned countryman Dr. Cave, in his literary history, calls this forgery a glaring lie. It is *always* ranked among the *spurious* works attributed to St. Jerome, in all the best editions of that Father, and abounds with such gross puerilities, absurdities, and anachronisms, that no one can imagine it to have proceeded from the pen of any man of ordinary intellect, much less would he ascribe the translation to St. Jerome, or the supposed Hebrew original (which no one ever saw) to an inspired Evangelist, St. Matthew. Now all this, and much more to the same purport, is prefixed to this spurious gospel in the edition of Fabricius, not one syllable of which, for very obvious reasons, is hinted at by the editor of the Apocryphal New Testament. This person, with what candour and fairness of criticism any one may judge, leaves his readers to imagine that it is a generally received and acknowledged part of the genuine works of St. Jerome, and consequently, though not received as canonical by the church, at least countenanced and supported by one of the greatest Latin Fathers.

The next book in this collection is the Protevangelion, which we are told in the table and introduction was brought by Postellus from the Levant, translated by him into Latin and sent to Oporinus, a printer at Basil, where Bibliander, a protestant divine and Professor of Divinity at Zurich, caused it to be printed in 1552. If the editor had informed his readers who Postellus was, he might perhaps have excited considerable doubts as to his credibility, when he asserts that " this Gospel was publicly read in the Eastern churches, they making no doubt that James was the author of it." However, since for very obvious reasons he has not done this, I will mention a few only, out of the innumerable extravagancies and impieties of this person.

William Postel was by birth a Norman, and was banished successively from France, Vienna, and Rome, for his singular and impious opinions. On the same account he was expelled from the order of the Jesuits, of which he was a member, imprisoned at Rome and Venice for his blasphemies, and only released because he was held to be a maniac, which was undoubtedly the case, and at last died in a monastery where he was confined. As a specimen of some of his opinions, it may suffice to say that he maintained he had been dead and had risen again ; that the soul of Adam had entered into his body ; that the angel Raziel had revealed to him the secrets of heaven ; and that his writings were dictated to him by Jesus Christ. Such is the man whose testimony is advanced as that of a grave and sober divine. It may not be improper to add that Bibliander, who caused this book to be printed, was deprived of his Professorship on account of his religious opinions.

It is farther stated in the introduction to the Protevangelion, "that the allusions to this gospel in the ancient Fathers are frequent, and their expressions indicate that it had obtained a very general credit in the Christian world." That " the controversies founded on it chiefly relate to the age of Joseph at the birth of Christ, and to his being a widower with children before his marriage with the Virgin." That " it seems material to remark that the legends of the latter age affirm the virginity of Joseph, notwithstanding Epiphanius, Hilary, Chrysostom, Cyril, Euthymius, Theophylact, Œcumenius, and indeed all the Latin Fathers till Ambrose, and the Greek Fathers afterwards, maintain the opinion of Joseph's age and family, founded upon their belief in the authenticity of this book."

In these remarks, a great host of witnesses, 'Fathers of the Church,' are brought forward to testify to the authenticity of the Protevangelion, and the inference necessarily to be deduced is, that with such a cloud of witnesses, either the book must be genuine, or at least that they who believed this book to be genuine, and believed the other scriptures also, must have seen nothing in *them* superior in style or importance to the contents of *this*, and must have placed it on a level with them. In other words, that they must have been unable to detect this book to be spurious from any internal evidence, and consequently that the value of their testimony to the truth of the canonical scriptures is to be appreciated from their estimation of this; that is to say, their credulity in this case being exposed, the value of their testimony to the truth of the genuine gospels is hardly worth consideration.

I will first instance some of the puerile and idle conceits, some of the stupid and anile absurdities of this book, and then examine how far the statement of its being generally believed by such a host of Fathers is correct. We are told in Ch. vi. that Mary at nine months old walked nine steps, and then came back to her mother's lap, who said that she should walk no more till she was brought to the temple of the Lord. In Ch. vii. we are informed that at three years old her father Joachim took her to the temple, and the high priest placed her on the third step of the altar, where the Lord gave her grace, and she danced with her feet. We are farther gravely informed that she continued in the temple till twelve years old, receiving her food from the hand of an angel. That the priests then consulted about finding a husband for her, and that they were ordered by an angel to call all the widowers together, each of whom was to bring a rod with him; that Joseph came among them, and that a dove flew out of his rod and flew upon the head of Joseph, who was thereupon chosen to betroth the Virgin, which he refused, being an old man, and was then compelled to take her. We have then an account of the Salutation, partly copied from St. Luke, with some embellishments. We are then informed that at the birth of Christ, Joseph went to seek a Hebrew midwife, and saw the fowls stopping in their flight, the working people at their food not moving, those who had meat at their mouths not eating, those who lifted their hands to their heads not taking them away; the sheep dispersed but standing still; the kids, with their mouths to the water, at the river, and touching it but not drinking. We have then an account of Salome's hand withering, for not believing that a Virgin had brought forth, and restored by touching the child ; a mountain opening miraculously to hide John and his mother Elizabeth at the murder of the Innocents; the roofs of the temple howling at the murder of Zacharias, and his blood turned into a stone. This is the Gospel which such a host of Fathers are stated to have believed. Now let us see how true this statement is.

Origen, Tom. XI. in Matth, p. 223, says, " *Some affirm* that the brothers of Jesus were the sons of Joseph by a former wife, being led to this *by the tradition* of the gospel which is inscribed that according to Peter, or the book of James." Now when Origen says *some affirm*, and talks of *the tradition* of the gospel, the only possible inference is that *he did not* affirm this, and *did not* believe that gospel to be genuine. For if he had believed it, he must have said, not *some affirm*, but *we find*, or *we learn*, and he must have called this *not a traditionary* gospel, but quoted it as genuine and authentic.

Epiphanius, who flourished about A. D. 368, and whom we have just seen quoted as a believer by the editor of these Apocryphal Gospels, says that the Ebionites, by whom this pretended gospel was written, in order to gain credit for their forgeries, falsify the names of the Apostles, with which they inscribe some of their forged books ; for instance, with the name of *James* (alluding to this very book), and of *Matthew* (alluding to the preceding Gospel of Mary), and of the other disciples.

Eustathius, Bishop of Antioch, about A. D. 325, calls the writer of this book. *one* James. A term sufficient to convince any one he did not mean James the Apostle.

Epiphanius the Presbyter A. D. 519, says, that they who have attempted to give an account of the life of the Virgin Mary have proceeded ill, and have condemned themselves, such as *James the Hebrew*, and Aphrodisian the Persian, and certain others. Where by his use of the term James *the Hebrew*, and coupling him with Aphrodisian *the Persian*, it is clear that he also could not mean to attribute this book to the Apostle St. James.

As to the learned men who lived when this book was first produced by Postellus and published by Bibliander, and who have written since that time, they are unanimous in rejecting it, to do which indeed no learning is necessary, nor any qualification beyond that of common sense; but it is important to observe, with regard to the observation of Postellus, that this book " was generally received and read in the Eastern Churches," that there does not appear to be any satisfactory foundation for this, nor does he bring any proof beyond his own assertion. What credit is to be given to that, I have already shewn by a short sketch of his life and character.

You will easily perceive, my Reverend Brethren, that it is impossible to go through the whole contents of the publication in question, within the limits of an address like the present, nor indeed is it necessary. The tracts contain their own refutation, and it would be a waste of time to enter into an elaborate examination of them all. When they were published by Fabricius, they were accompanied with an antidote to their poison, extracted from the writings of the most eminent scholars and divines ; they were open to scholars, who alone are capable of making a proper use of them, and they were inaccessible to the ignorant and ill-disposed. The purpose of the present editor cannot be mistaken. He has artfully assumed the appearance of candour, and has appropriated, with some learning and more dexterity, so much of the prolegomena of Fabricius as seemed suitable to his purpose ; the rest he has kept back ; and while the avowed object of his publication is merely to illustrate the arts, " and render an acceptable service to the theological student and ecclesiastical antiquary," to both of whom, be it remembered, these apocryphal writings were accessible before, in the edition of Fabricius, his real design is to lower the canonical scriptures in the estimation of ignorant and uneducated persons, by presenting to them, as nearly as possible in the same form, divisions, and style of language, these Apocryphal writings, and thus to perplex their judgment and unsettle their faith.

In order to carry his pernicious design still more effectually into practice, he has subjoined the Apostles' creed in its antient state, copied from a note in Mr. Justice Bailey's edition of the Common Prayer, and contrasted with the same creed in the usual editions of our Common Prayer-book. The reader is thus naturally induced to suppose that the learned Judge has disapproved of the Apostles' creed in its usual form, whereas the note merely states, what no one questions, that " it is not to be understood

that the Apostles' Creed was framed by the Apostles, or existed
as a Creed in their time." It is then given in its earliest form,
as it existed prior to the year 600. The authorities for this
are quoted, and then is subjoined the following important observation, which any fair and well meaning editor ought to have
produced, and which the Editor of the Apocryphal Gospels, finding
that he could not insert it without wholly destroying the insinua-
tion he wished to convey, has wilfully, I may add fraudulently,
omitted. The words are these: " the additions were probably
made *in opposition to particular heresies and opinions.*" I have
printed the latter part of this sentence in Italics, because it clearly
shews that in the learned writer's mind no objection existed to
these additions. Then follow the Apostolical Fathers as they
are called, the genuineness of whose works however is in many —
cases doubtful, and in some highly questionable. They are given
in Archbishop Wake's translation, on whom the highest praise is
bestowed, it suiting the editor in this instance to forget the declam-
ations about Hierarchs and Shrine-makers contained in his preface.
In this portion of his publication the editor seems to have aimed
at obtaining countenance for the former part, by bringing forward
the highly respectable names of an English Judge and Archbishop,
trusting to the inexperience of those for whom his publication is
designed, to confound the intentions of these eminent and pious
persons with his own, and thus fraudulently sheltering himself
under their sanction and approbation.

I might say much on this head, did the time permit, but

E

I think it sufficient to have pointed out the tendency and object of this insidious publication. No man can mistake these. With all the appearance of candour and fairness, with all the plausibility of impartial detail, and all the parade of learned references, any scholar who examines the book, who knows the sources from which the prefaces and illustrations are drawn, who sees not only *what* is brought forward but *how* it is brought forward, and who also knows what is suppressed and *why* it is suppressed, cannot but come to the inevitable conclusion that " AN ENEMY HATH DONE THIS."

Permit me now to add a few words on the possibility of extracting good out of this intended evil.

Whoever is at the pains of examining these apocryphal writings, cannot but be struck with their amazing inferiority to the canonical books. Even the writings of the Apostolical Fathers, which, whether genuine or not, have a much greater claim to our attention than the apocryphal gospels, when they depart from the model and language of the real apostolical and scriptural writings, which for the most part they closely copy, admit of no comparison with them. But in fact these writings of the Apostolical Fathers are so far valuable to us, as being unquestionably of a very early age, and written on the model of the genuine Apostolical Epistles. Where they coincide with *these*, therefore, they tend to prove *their* authenticity, and *their* early reception into the canon of Scripture, in which it is clear they must have had a place prior to those writings which are professed imitations of them. To take by far the most important of them all, the first Epistle of Clement to the Corinthians. The greater part of this book is a close, and sometimes almost a literal imitation of Saint Paul's epistles, or a transcript of the Psalms, or of some other parts of the Old or New Testament, applied by the way of exhortation to the persons addressed in the epistle. And so far as the writer adheres to his inspired prototypes he does well, and is indeed valuable to us, as confirming, by his innumerable quotations and manifest allusions, the authenticity of the present canonical scriptures. Be it remembered also, he quotes the Epistle of St. James, which was one of those latest received into the settled canon of scripture, and the Epistle of St. Paul to the Hebrews. So far then the first Epistle of Clement, which whether genuine or not is certainly of very high antiquity, is very valuable; but we cannot fail to be struck with the exceeding disparity between this book and the genuine text of Scripture, if we compare them in the first passage of any length, in which the writer forsakes his archetype and writes from his own resources. It may be worth while to examine the passage for the sake of making the comparison.

He is adducing analogies to illustrate the resurrection; and, after glancing at St. Paul's arguments, he continues thus—

"Let us consider that wonderful type of the resurrection which is seen in the Eastern Countries, that is to say in Arabia. There is a certain bird called a Phœnix: of this there is never but one

at a time, and that lives five hundred years. And when the time
of its dissolution draws near, that it must die, it makes itself a
nest of frankincense and myrrh and other spices, into which (when
its time is fulfilled) it enters and dies. But its flesh putrifying
breeds a certain worm, which, being nourished with the juice of
the dead bird, brings forth feathers, and when it is grown to a
perfect state it takes up the nest in which the bones of its parent
lie, and carries it from Arabia into Egypt, to a city called Heliopolis,
and flying in the open day, in the sight of all men, lays it upon
the altar of the sun, and so returns from whence it came. The
priests then search into the records of time, and find that it
returned precisely at the end of five hundred years.

Suffer me to quote, familiar as they must be to you, in contrast
to this childish and idle tale, the words of St. Paul illustrative of
the same awful subject. *" But some men will say how are the
dead raised up, and with what body do they come? Thou
fool, that which thou sowest is not quickened except it die,
and that which thou sowest, thou sowest not that body that
shall be, but bare grain, it may chance of wheat or of some
other grain; but God giveth it a body as it hath pleased
him, and to every seed his own body. All flesh is not the
same flesh. But there is one kind of flesh of men, another
flesh of beasts, another of fishes, and another of birds. There
are also celestial bodies and bodies terrestrial, but the glory
of the celestial is one, and the glory of the terrestrial is
another. There is one glory of the sun, and another glory of
the moon, and another glory of the stars, for one star differeth*

from another star in glory. So also is the resurrection of the dead. It is sown in corruption, it is raised in incorruption; it is sown in weakness, it is raised in power; it is sown a natural body, it is raised a spiritual body. There is a natural body and there is a spiritual body, and so it is written; the first man Adam was made a living soul, the last Adam was made a quickening spirit. Howbeit that was not first which is spiritual, but that which is natural, and afterward that which is spiritual. The first man is of the earth, earthy: the second man is the Lord from heaven. As is the earthy, such are they that are earthy, and as is the heavenly, such are they also that are heavenly. And as we have borne the image of the earthy, we shall also bear the image of the heavenly." Who of you, my brethren, does not hear in the former of these passages, the feeble and fallacious language of human imbecility, in the latter the all powerful and soul awakening voice of unerring inspiration? But all comment on such a contrast is superfluous.

Again, in one of these Apocryphal Gospels, that of Infancy, we are told (ch. xx. 15) that our Saviour was brought to school, and that " when the master lifted up his hand to whip him, his hand presently withered, and he died. Then said Joseph to *Saint* Mary—Henceforth we will not allow him to go out of the house, for every one who displeases him is killed." Let us now hear the words of truth (Luke ix. 52). "*And he sent messengers before his face, and they went and entered into a village of the Samaritans to make ready for him. And*

*they did not receive him because his face was as though he
would go to Jerusalem.   And when his disciples James and
John saw this, they said, Lord, wilt thou that we command
fire to come down from heaven and consume them as Elias
did?   But he turned and rebuked them, and said, ye know
not what manner of spirit ye are of; for the Son of man is
not come to destroy mens' lives but to save them."*

One instance more out of a thousand and I will conclude
this topic.   In the Gospel of Infancy (Ch. xix. 22), we read,
" Another time, when the Lord Jesus was coming home in the
evening with Joseph, he met a boy, who ran so hard against
him that he threw him down.   To whom the Lord Jesus said,
as thou hast thrown me down, so shalt thou fall, nor ever rise.
And that moment the boy fell down and died."   Now hear
St. Luke, xxiii. 33.   *" And when they were come to a place
which is called Calvary, there they crucified him, and the
malefactors, one on the right hand and the other on the left.
Then said Jesus, Father, forgive them, for they know not
what they do."*

Such is the splendid contrast between the genuine Gospels
and these spurious imitations, a contrast which might be carried
to a great extent, even through the whole of these apocryphal
writings, but of which it is quite sufficient to have adduced these
few instances.   There are however two great points, in which
good may be extracted from the intended evil.   First, as the
original must have existed before the copy, these spurious gospels,

where they copy and follow the genuine scriptures, bear testimony to the priority of their existence; and secondly, where they do not copy them, but relate, as some do, rabbinical traditions for revealed truths, or detail such miracles as the invention of the writer could supply, they only serve to place the genuine scripture miracles and the character of our blessed. Lord, as recorded by his real Evangelists, his faithful followers and eye-witnesses of the truth, in a still more striking and splendid point of view. We are apt, perhaps, by our familiarity with the genuine scriptures, not always to feel the full force and beauty of what is recorded for our instruction or imitation. We are so accustomed to see *nothing but* perfection in the character of Christ, *nothing but* almighty power in his miracles, and goodness in his example, that we perhaps dwell less on the particular instances than we ought, and have our perceptions in these cases somewhat blunted by habit. But the instant we begin to contrast them with the spurious character and false miracles contained in these apocryphal books, all the keenness of our perception is restored, we are at once awakened to reflection, we catch by intuition, and pursue with avidity, the train of thought and argument which leads us to a sure conviction of the truth of the genuine scriptures, and the rejection of the apocryphal, founded on the internal evidence of each. In the former we recognize all that is simple, elevated, and divine, in the latter nothing but human follies, human frailities, and human infirmities.

A just and close enquiry into the external evidences of these writings will lead to a similar conclusion as to the truth of the one and the spuriousness of the other. I have touched upon this already in a former part of this address ; it is far too extensive a subject to pursue now, but I can only say, upon my own experience, that the closer and more critical the enquiry is into the authenticity of the received Canon of Scripture, the stronger will the evidence be in its favour, and the more decisive to the exclusion of the rejected books. But another most important inference resulting from this enquiry must not be passed over. It is quite clear that the received canonical books of scripture contain all things necessary to our salvation, and notwithstanding the opinion of the very learned Michaelis, I confess I see but little reason to think that any writings of St. Paul, which could at all claim to have been classed among the canonical books, have been lost. The original compilers of the Canon of Scripture seem, as I have already stated, to have collected from time to time the various writings of the Apostles and Evangelists as fast as they were written and circulated, and of course soon after the death of St. John, the latest of these writers, that is, about the end of the first or beginning of the second century, the collection must have been complete. It seems hardly probable that the writings of so eminent an apostle as St. Paul could have escaped the notice, or, being noticed, could have been purposely omitted among the collected Scriptures of the primitive Christian Church, unless indeed they were of a nature different from those which are preserved to us, and written, if I may use the expression, in his private, not in his apostolic character. That several such might exist is by no means impossible, or indeed improbable, and if they did, it is a strong proof of the caution of the primitive Church, that its rulers were not led even by the sanction of so high and venerable a name, to admit any thing as canonical scripture which did not bear the marks of genuine Apostolic authority.

That the collection thus formed was not recognized by a Christian Council earlier than that of Nice, is accounted for by this plain and unanswerable argument, that we knew of no Christian Council earlier, and it is proved indisputably, that although not confirmed by a Christian Council, the collection was received in the Christian Church, long before that period, in its present form.

One inference, therefore, is, that we have *all* the genuine Scriptures, as well as all that are necessary to our salvation. Another, and no less important, is, that among the Apocryphal books which have come down to us, there is not one which has the least claim to be received as genuine. We are therefore sure that we have received nothing but what we ought to have received, and have rejected nothing but what we ought to have rejected. And having therefore these certain means of being made wise unto Salvation, let us earnestly endeavour to inculcate and impart this wisdom among our brethren, and the members of those flocks which are respectively committed to our care; for *blessed is that servant whom our Lord at his coming shall find so doing; of a truth I say unto you that he will make him ruler over all that he hath.*

EDDOWES, PRINTER, SHREWSBURY.

CPSIA information can be obtained
at www.ICGtesting.com
Printed in the USA
BVHW020108140421
604867BV00002B/9

* 9 7 8 1 1 6 7 1 6 1 9 1 9 *